The TOPSY Turvy KING

ALISON BREWIS / HANNAH GREEN

Jesus had disciples,
his friends who followed him.
He told them he was God's King
who'd come to deal with sin.

Then one day his disciples
were having quite a fight.
They wanted to be greatest
and each thought he was right.

But Jesus told them,

"The

BIG

must be

the
small.

A king

must be
a servant.

And I

will serve
you all."

His friends were all astounded.
Their brains just nearly burst!

"We think he might be crazy.

He's a topsy turvy King!

Or else this topsy turvy man
makes sense of everything!"

All the friends had gathered
to have some food to eat,
when Jesus took some water
and began to wash their feet.

"We think he might be crazy.
He's a topsy turvy King!
Or else this topsy turvy man
makes sense of everything!"

But on a sad, sad Friday
some soldiers killed their King.
He looked like he was nothing,
not Lord of everything.

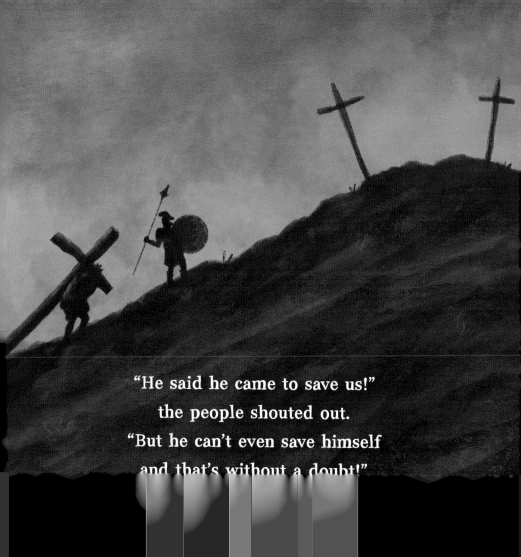

"He said he came to save us!"
the people shouted out.
"But he can't even save himself
and that's without a doubt!"

"We thought he might be crazy.
He was a topsy turvy King!
Or else this topsy turvy man
made sense of everything!"

It seemed their King was beaten.
He lay dead in a tomb.
Had God rejected Jesus
and left him in the gloom?

But when the sun came shining,
that happy Easter day

Jesus was alive again
and he was here to stay!

"My Kingdom is
quite different.

In fact it's
upside down!"

The dying,
saving servant

is the one who
wears the crown!

"We thought he might be crazy.
He's a topsy turvy King!

Jesus is King of the whole world,
but he came to earth with a surprising
job to do. He came to die on the cross,
taking the punishment we deserve for
turning away from God. Now Jesus is
alive again and if we trust in Jesus to
forgive us, we can be friends with God.
A King who came to rescue us?
Well that's topsy turvy good news!

Jesus "did not come to be served, but to serve, and to give his life as a ransom for many."

MARK 10:45

For Nicholas, Ana,
Isabelle and Sebastian

ISBN: 978-1-914966-67-5

Published by 10Publishing, a division of 10ofThose Limited,
Tomlinson Road, Leyland, Lancs, PR25 2DY, England
info@10ofthose.com
www.10ofthose.com

Written by Alison Brewis
Illustrated by Hannah Green
Designed by Diane Warnes

Publishing
a division of 10 of those.com

10Publishing is committed to publishing
quality Christian resources that are biblical,
accessible and point people to Jesus.

www.10ofthose.com is our online retail partner
selling thousands of quality books at discounted prices.

For information contact: info@10ofthose.com
or check out our website: www.10ofthose.com